Fall Risk

Fall Risk
New & Selected Poems
Bill McCarthy

GRAYSON BOOKS
West Hartford, Connecticut
graysonbooks.com

Fall Risk
Copyright © 2022 by Bill McCarthy
Published by Grayson Books
West Hartford, Connecticut
ISBN: 978-0-9838603-4-1
Library of Congress Control Number: 2022914611

Book design by Cindy Stewart

Dedicated to my friend and editor, Rick Sale. He opened a new door for me when he published my first chapbook, Past Sins, the thirtieth in the annual series—*Contemporary Poets Reading*—sponsored by the Friends of the University of North Texas Libraries. I remain deeply grateful.

Acknowledgments

I thank my friends, Patrick-Pesek Herriges and Irl Carter for their consistent encouragement and support, and in particular, Katie Cooney, who worked with me on version after version. Thanks to Kate Smith and Betsy Meyer, who made creative recommendations as they assembled the constantly morphing manuscript. And most especially, thank you to my wife, Danette. She not only helped make room in our lives for creating this book, but frequently made deceptively small recommendations that, time and again, had a profound impact on the final work.

The following poems were previously published by Trilobite Press: "Ernestine," "Chasing Clouds on Horseback," "Past Sins," "Storm Riders," "Indra's Net," and "You're Leaving." "Breast Cancer Poem," originally titled "Breast Cancer Poem #2" was first published by *Main Channel Voices* and was nominated for a Pushcart Prize. The poem was also part of the anthology *Cancer Poetry Project 2*, which *Midwest Book Awards* named Best Poetry Book.

"Gappa" is for Jamison McCarthy

"Dani" is for Danette McCarthy

"Patricia" for Mary Catherine Snyder, in memory of her mother.

"Return to Innisfree" is in memory of John V. McCarthy

"Sailing Alone" is for Katie Cooney

"Rock Chant" is for Maggie Kessell

"In Lieu of Flowers" is in memory of Pat Enright

Contents

I.

Purpose

Just keep walking.
Trust each foot
to find
the next flat stone
already beneath it.

Your newfound
path—
it has been
waiting patiently
for a lifetime,
or more.

Covenant vs. Credo

"And I am not afraid to make a mistake,
even a great mistake, a lifelong mistake
and perhaps as long as eternity too."
—from *A Portrait of the Artist as a Young Man*
by James Joyce

It takes courage to live without
creed or credo—
no man-made walls to sleep within.
No roof to keep out the rain.
But such a roof can also blind us
    to the beauty of the stars.

Why not choose to live from covenant?

Be willing to listen to songs sung in many voices.
Recognize the complete inadequacy of mere tolerance,
and instead, replace it with authentic respect
    and deep compassion.

Dick the Potter

How many of us wear out body parts
    doing what we love?

Mostly we let the sun ravage our skin,
allow age to take out our knees and,
perhaps, let alcohol scar our livers.

Dick is a potter who has worn out his thumbs
    creating pieces of functional beauty.

Coffee mugs with beautifully shaped lips
    and gently curved handles.
Platters whose elegant glazes seem to ask
    to be passed,
piled with the most succulent of entrées.

Dick has no regrets.

Hundreds of pieces from his hands live in
    the homes of the most discerning.
People who understand the power of beauty
    to transform the very environment itself.

You see, Dick's work is so much more than clay.

They enter as artifacts but become members
    of the family.
They speak to who we are and what we love
    and cherish.
What more could one ask?

Birches and Oaks

Birch trees live too close together for my liking.
So straight and smooth; so much the same.
You just know they're hiding something
beneath that papery, alabaster skin.

I'll take an oak any day.
It has the good sense to demand
some breathing room. Like sturdy
Norwegians, oaks keep their counsel.
But when they burn, it goes long and hot.
Too bad so much is left unsaid before the saw.

Beliefs

Beliefs can be dangerous when
they masquerade as facts—
solid, cold, and true.

But breathe on them and they can
shimmer like jello. Drop them, and
they fracture like mercury, scattering
silver BBs too toxic to touch.

Beliefs ought to require a warning label:

Danger
Do not operate if using alcohol, drugs,
  or taking oneself too seriously.

Morning at the Feeder

An unruly gang of blue jays rummages for oilers
in the snow beneath the feeder, coming and going,
hopping and swooping back to the nearby birches.

A hairy woodpecker travels up and down the post
like an old-fashioned wooden toy on a string.
The nuthatch clowns upside down on the feeder
box because it can.

All the while black-capped chickadees fill in
behind the others until an incoming jay explodes
onto the speckled snow, sending chickadees
outward like feathered shrapnel.

Losing Our Religion

We're without religion again.
I thought it was tied on real good,
but maybe it worked its way loose
and fell out of your brother's red Ford pickup.

Your brother. He wouldn't lift a single
box until the end of the Bears-Packers
game and even then, he wasn't worth
a shit because his Bears lost and he couldn't
seem to rant and work at the same time.

I've never been good at knots.
I once lost an entire relationship
off a pier because my string of
half-hitches didn't hold.

Maybe if I hadn't gotten kicked out of
cub scouts, I'd know my knots and I'd
be tied on good and tight to some god
who doesn't let the first mean curve
pitch him from the truck.

Faith

When I was small,
every other spring or so,
my father set fire to the field
behind our house to burn off
the dead weeds and dried grasses.

I'd watch him out there,
a blue bandana tied over his mouth,
yellow-white smoke curling ahead of him.
He'd dig into the mounds of old grass
with a long-tined fork so the flames
could get a good lick at them.

That blackened field looked empty for a while.
Then you'd start to notice a few green vines,
gopher mounds, and last summer's baseball.
They'd all been hiding in the old weeds and grasses.

In a couple of weeks, wind and rain would
flush away the charred vegetation.
Already the brilliant green was inching up.
It was like you couldn't hold it back
if you wanted to.
And it always seemed to come back better,
better than it was before.

It's times like these I could really use
the faith of my father.

What Will It Take?

In the dark, you think it's a few leaves cartwheeling
on their points across the pavement.
But then, your headlights reflect in an eye and you
recognize the distinctive hop plop hop—
an army of leopard frogs
is migrating across the highway.

First, you dodge; you swerve.
But there are hundreds of them.
Save one; sacrifice ten. So, you steel yourself,
stare beyond the pool of light, and just drive.

My grandfather had been an engineer
on the Great Northern Railroad.
Sprawled in the corner of Grandma's couch, he told
me about a trip he made through Montana.
During the night, thousands of frogs
were migrating across the tracks.

As the coal-fired engine pulled its load up a grade,
the wheels began to slip, grinding round and
round on the grease from small green-brown bodies.
Then, with a final exhale, his engine coughed to a halt
in the pitch darkness.

Bodies. Thousands and thousands of bodies.
It calls to mind chapters in our human history.
Gettysburg, thousands of soldiers dead in just
three days. World War I, millions dead. World War II,
over twice as many soldiers and civilians as WWI.
Vietnam, over a million dead. And Rwanda,
an estimated 800,000 in 100 days of genocide.

Remember, once upon a time, somewhere
in the dark near Billings,
surrounded by a moving carpet of green and brown,
a mountain of iron sat silently among the deep night sounds.

Letting Go

The river winds
through its rocky channel
tumbling over boulders,
delighting in the moment,
unconcerned that the coming falls
always shatters it into a million jewels.

Obituary

Are you among those whose parents' waves are now cresting?
Do you notice celebrity names from their generation in obituaries?
We can see the span of their lives rising, and eventually
crashing onto the shore,
releasing pieces we can put together that tell the story of
who they were and the difference they made.

"touched the lives of 1000's;" "creative innovator;"
"a doer, rooted in faith;" "married the love of her life;"
"lover of ideas and questions;" "unselfish kindness."

"served in respected leadership;" "master sculptor;"
"avid skier and speed skater;" "they were the best of friends;"
"will be deeply missed;" "fiercely independent till the end."

In due time we too will feel the water roll up from its flat trough,
carrying us to our wave's inevitable white crest,
and as it breaks, revealing our own complex legacy
of love and loss; joy and regret.

Hopefully, it will leave memories on a shore where our loved
ones can meet, gather them up, and join these memories into
personal maps and inspired stories.
Stories that will help them navigate their own journeys
on this ever-changing sea.

The Water Strider

What occupies us day to day is so small.
What truly matters is a mystery.

We are like the water strider, skating
on water's skin, its world a mere molecule
deep, separated from unknowable depths
that fall off cool and quiet, ageless and
enormous, just beneath it.

I believe it is water, not dust to which
we shall return, and only then to learn what
has truly mattered since the beginning.

II.

Waiting For the Sun

It's January.
Windows closed.
I no longer wake up
to the voices of flycatcher,
robin, and mourning dove.

The few birds still here,
mostly black and white,
wake up to my light
already lit, and together,
we wait for the sun.

Ice Out

Crows dot the frozen lake
out near the center of the bay.
They walk stiff-legged like old
men in baggy pants.

The fish houses have been removed
and the crows gab and peck at dried
minnows and broken Fritos on their
patch of rotting ice.

Soon the ice will honeycomb
beneath its thin covering of
snow, and herring gulls and terns
will join the feast on open water.

Gappa

From my living room chair I hear a two-year-old's pajama-
softened feet pattering down the hall's hardwood floor. Then,
like a dam breach, his energy floods the morning room,
spreading into every corner, competing with the sun itself.

Two ancient cats leap for the safety of higher ground.
It's as though this new green day was created just for him.
Everything returns the smile of his laughter.

Whatever concerns may have darkened my mind on waking
have been been washed away.
How could I have known my new name—Gappa—
would so completely melt my heart.

Snapshots

I love those snapshots of guys
back in the '60s,
barely 20 years old, white t-shirt
with sleeves rolled up,
leaning on a Chevy or a Fairlane,
a Lucky or Camel dangling
from a cool-ass grin.

Those saplings are now encircled
by decades of rings—
'Nam and Nixon,
kids and grandkids.
You may not always see it,
but don't think for a moment
that the grin is gone.

Mickey's Diner

It's Thursday evening. Nearly closing.
The big man has been waiting tables here
since I showed up in town years ago.

As Jack stacks up plates, I ask, "How
goes it?" He grunts something unintelligible
and then says clearly. "Depressed.

Waiting on two surgeries. The ankle.
It never did heal after the fall."
And the back? "Doctors say I'll be laid
up four months or better."

His brother came to town last week.
First time since their mother's funeral.
"That was nice. Family's nice."
But he sure misses his daughter.

Loaded down with empty plates and
glasses, Jack steers toward the kitchen.
Navigating around empty tables,
he cuts across shoals of regret.

An aging river tug makes its last,
lone run of the day.

Dani

Her energy is an inexorable river
that predictably breaches its banks.
Draws in small children and pets,
roils with old lovers and new friends.

We smile and laugh through the rapids,
launching bravely over the falls. Not only
does no one get hurt, but some walk away
with a quiet confidence they had never known.

Ernestine

I find it hard to believe,
my mother and father
clowning for the camera,
but there they are, fixed in time.

Back-to-back, arms interlocked,
shirtless in khakis, he bends forward,
drawing her across his back.
Her loose cotton dress rides up.
She's laughing.

This lightness had all but drained away when I arrived.
I watched them age through their fifties and beyond,
but never learned what they desired.
What makes parents show up like empty paint cans?
Where are the skies they have painted?

Ernestine sits vigil in her wheelchair.
It's mid-afternoon, and attendants in flowered scrubs
drift past her door.
She's 91. Her husband is dead.
The photographer is dead.
Only she remains, suspended between a clouding past
and shrinking present.

Draped across the back of her boyfriend,
legs dangling loosely in the afternoon,
does this girl of summer ever visit my mother
in her dreams?

St. Joseph's Cafeteria Song

Go to your locker first.
Get your lunch.
Come immediately to the cafeteria.
People are not to congregate in the lavatory.
Freshmen should be at the cafeteria by 11:33.
No singing is permitted.

Each girl must have two napkins every lunch period.
One for table use; one for personal use.
A penalty of 25 cents will be imposed
after the first failure to observe the practice.
Remember, singing is never permitted.

Use doors marked "in" and "out."
Take your lunch out of the brown paper bag.
Crush the bag into a small ball and put it
in the receptacle provided.
Wipe up what you have spilled.
And don't forget, no singing is ever permitted.

The Monarch

The monarch's flight,
so quietly random.
So giddy. Each stroke,
a seeming surprise. Like
divining the next
digit
of pi.

Those People

Where do they come from?
Those special people who appear,
and because of who they are,
change our lives forever.

The ones who made outrageous
requests and always, always
expected our best, not realizing
we weren't as talented as the rest,
but we simply couldn't let them down.

The ones who invited us to play
though we were about to walk away
because we felt we didn't fit. They said,
"stay," and we stayed, and played
and before too long, we did belong.

Be sure the list includes the ones we told
when we were afraid and feeling cold.
They touched us, smiled, and said,
"you'll do the right thing, kid,"
and when that day came, we did.

They're small in number but big in heart
and each has played such an important part
in whom we are, and whom we will become.
How they find us, it's hard to say, but let's
just be grateful it turned out that way.

Patricia

Year by year the cancer seemed to
shrink her body until she became
so slight, you might think you could
hold her in one hand, and the puff
of your breath would send her small
frame tumbling like a leaf.

But still, she would wade, without
hesitation, into a choppy sea of politics
and religion, rarely with judgment,
always with curiosity, making it safe for
the most reluctant to begin the long
swim out of the shallows of intolerance,
toward the deeper waters of justice and
compassion.

Black Irish

My mother said he was "black Irish,"
one of those Irishman born dark of temperament.
Not like our neighbor, O'Kane—full of bull and
blarney, who likely as not would be telling jokes
and singing "Danny Boy" if you gave him half a pint.

Albert and I shared the same sky, but our orbits seldom crossed.
Long before I arrived, he had raised and launched three sons
and now seemed ready to be finished with fathering.
A contained man, I approached him neither for money nor
counsel.

But in my mid-20s, I lost my way and crashed to earth.
My silent father reached across the chasm between us—
his hand-written letter held up a journeyman printer's life,
honest work that had served him for decades.

I deeply resented this intrusion into my personal chaos.
Who was he to suggest such a commonplace path?
I never acknowledged his letter.
He never questioned my silence.
Only decades later—the father of an adult son myself—
did I glimpse what it took to extend that invitation.

Note: The term "Black Irish," is commonly used to describe Irish people with
dark hair and dark eyes. The popular origin story is the intermarriage with
Spaniards who fought beside the Irish against the British in the 17th century.

The Potted Hibiscus

Early May. The newly purchased
hothouse hibiscus, price tag dangling,
sits regally on the corner of the deck.

What has this princess-like plant
with its flamboyant blooms done
to earn a midwestern spring?
Has it gone to sleep, died,
and been reborn? Not a chance.

This naive girl, all dressed
for prom, likely believes all
is sunshine when you want it
and rain when you need it. Hah!
Welcome to Minnesota, my dear!

Chasing Clouds on Horseback

She said her favorite thing back then was to
ride her horse flat-out across the prairie,
chasing squall clouds that trailed showers
like the tendrils of a jellyfish.

Most days the air was so dry, the rain
never touched the ground.
But sometimes they would catch one
hanging very low, and its cold drops
would mix with dust, sweat, and hair,
creating tears she still can taste.

The Red-Tailed Hawk

I.
I remember her warning— "Let your brother be!"
But I'd pad up the steps anyway and slip into his
bedroom before dawn, a waggling pup drawn
to the scent of last night's adventure that clings
to the sleeping hound.

II.
I remember the itch and odor of army surplus wool
as we rumbled home from hunting in his mid-50s
blue Ford. A few stiffening squirrels and rabbits
bumped in the trunk with a scuffed leather Dopp kit,
spare socks, and an orphaned tee shirt—all
corroborating evidence of his portable bachelor life.

Mostly we rode in silence; there was little to be said.
The drone of the heater fan drew me out over
sleepy shoals into deeper water where pieces
of this day settle through layer after layer,
anchoring more securely than memory itself.

III.
I stand on my weathered cedar deck nursing a coffee
in the pre-dawn haze, too little light to waken sleeping
colors. Six small birds are silhouetted on the skeleton
of a jack pine over fifty yards away.

The angle of a tail, the way one fidgets on a branch,
the shrug of another as it preens—like the gardener
who knows his plants from their first shoots, or the
mother who easily picks her child from scores of tiny
bodies on a beach—thanks to him, I can identify each
bird without the benefit of sound or color.

IV.

He would not fail to notice the broad arc
of the red-tailed hawk—a feathered samurai—
settle silently onto a roadside power pole.
Tell me. What is worth knowing?
What do we take the time to see?

Black Cherry Tree

Tiny purple jewels,
mostly pit,
that August wasps
wait to ripen
then surround
with their
gold and black
bodies. Shivering
drunkards, they
drain the fermented
sweetness until all
the meat is gone
and only the wooden
pearl remains
like a dry eyeball,
still attached, but
waiting for frost
to drop and deliver
on the slim promise
of a new tree.

Past Sins

Years back I ran a truck through the
middle of my life, leaving splintered
bones poking through skin like white
plastic straws stuck into soft ground.

By the time I came to, the red blood
spatter had turned brown and
bruises had begun to fade.

The truck still rests on its side at the
bottom of a nearby ravine. The facts are
badly rusted and even eyewitnesses tell
different stories as to what sent it over
the edge on such a fine spring day.

III.

Storm Riders

You were eight, maybe nine. Wanting to be safe,
tempted by being scared, half hoping a twister
might coil out of the purple-black wall cloud
marching toward us from the west.

We hauled the straight-backed chairs
past the dining room's lace curtains, out onto
the concrete slab we called a front porch.
Breaking the inside rules, we propped those chairs
on their hind legs side by side against the wall,
a pair of fearless cowpokes sitting easy in some
nameless western town, waiting, just waiting with
steely patience for the summer storm bellowing off
in the west beyond the street maples
and tidy two-story houses.

Its voice was low and rumbling.
We could smell its green breath as the pause
between flash and crash quickened.
You shifted in your chair when the streetlamps
kicked on as the afternoon's hazy light was
swallowed into the storm's widening mouth.

The gate of rain swung open, pocking the roof
of our aging yellow Chrysler with wet hoof prints.
The wind blew up, swirling street sand and cold spray,
lashing like a spirit tongue, finally driving us inside
as hail hammered against walls and windows.

Our trusty chairs were returned to their rightful stalls.
We dried our faces on a clean dishtowel.
This was no defeat.
We rode that horse clean to the buzzer.

Gato

The stub-tailed cat eyes me from the doorway,
then plods tiger-like into the room
where we are about to share a chair.

She makes the effortless launch, does her
circular dance then settles in, squeezed
between the padded arm and my right thigh.

Her head is near my hand, positioned to
collect the occasional stroke when I can
no longer resist her liquid fur.

She leans into my touch. Accepts all I offer.
She does not say, "Oh no, I couldn't, you're
too kind." Or, "No, no, that's more than I could ask for!"

And yet, for all her feline self-focus,
I am the beneficiary and she is my benefactor.

True Companion

In the beginning we are just friends.
Then this voice emerges,
"You have found her again."

We now walk hand in hand, re-learning
to live heart to heart on a path of rediscovery
for whatever miles remain.

On this soul's earthly journey,
you are my true companion.

Listening Shore

Ancient white pines betray a bare murmur of
morning breeze on this sunlit lakeside shore.

What could have caused the heavy, jagged waves
on the big lake that now rake
the shoreline at 45-degrees before drawing back
and disappearing onto the sand and gravel?

Perhaps these morning rollers are the legacy of a storm—
angry words that occurred last night, far out on the lake,
and only now are reaching this listening shore.

It's easy to underestimate the impact of our past.
Harsh words from a parent that create a squall in the mind,
the death of a loved one that produces a storm in the heart.

We may live among white caps during our childhood,
then as adults, crash and slam against the very
people we love and who love us during what appear
to be days of gentle breezes.

Some learn to allow the breakers to pass through
without fear, without damage.
They are content to watch the waves until the moon
 rises over the water, still as glass.

Leaving

To fit a new Maytag down the basement steps,
my father once removed the hand railing
and never replaced it.
For years my hand would close on empty air
as I reached for its support, especially in the dark.

We've known for months that you were leaving.
You turned your light down slowly
from bright white to just a glow
so we wouldn't notice the coming change.

Your fine light, your steady voice,
despite your best efforts,
we knew were leaving—
especially in the dark.

More Words

He thought if he could only explain—
explain how he really felt about her,
about them, the pain and confusion
would end.

But the word pile continued to grow.
Eventually, it became so high
they could no longer see each other.

River Vespers

Egrets drift in over the darkening river,
      lighting reverently onto bent branches.
White prayer flags spreading blessings
      to all beings.

In Its Own Time

Love winds through life's landscape,
      finding its own way.
They meet in the green, but it is not their time,
      and so cross rivers with different lovers,
each believing the other has been left behind.

      But the heart knows.

One day they find each other in a clearing
      where success and failure, fear and longing,
no longer entangle them.

They quiet the voices that chatter of difference,
      choosing instead
the reference of a common heart
      that has lived for decades in the glade
of friendship, waiting to be welcomed anew.

It is a truer self that now emerges from the
      alchemy of love's lessons.
They are blossoms open full wide.
      Breath by breath, side by side,
they turn their faces toward a common sun.

Willy the Bat

He and I have never actually met,
but I know Willy from his work.
He processes the evening's insects,
leaving a neat mound of discards
like kernels of black rice on the
concrete slab near the front door.

Ours is an easy alliance.
He's the night shift; I am the day.
He's production; I'm maintenance.
Maybe one of these days we'll meet
at shift change, share a smoke and
pictures of our kids, and swap stories
about the stupidity of management.

And maybe, just maybe, I'll suggest
we take in a ball game on his night off.
No, it won't happen—
you know, family and all.
Still, it's good to have a co-worker
you can really count on…
night after night after night.

The Kiss

I place a greeting kiss on your cheek
       still rosy from the cold,
but my hungry lips know they were barely
       a breath from yours.
They now wonder why I have settled for
       the taste of chamomile and citrus,
when it could have been lush red wine.

Wedding Poem

Falling in love is easy.
Staying in love can be hard.
You must let go again and again.
Never stop listening.
Keep being curious.

Most people give up and leave.
Many give up and stay.
The successful ones? They accept
that love is a practice.
They bend but do not break.

And when the time comes, they place
body and soul into a crucible
to willingly become a new version
of themselves, beyond what either
could ever have imagined.

Close Relationship

The blue vein coils across the top of
my hand like a nightcrawler after a rain.
Beneath it, four tendons fan out from
my wrist like the tines of a leaf rake.

When I slowly flex my fingers, the tines
rise and fall and the worm slides.
We've been at arm's length for decades.
I don't say, "Hello," nearly as often as I should.

Breaking the Fast

He hears her body rustling in the morning bed,
the sound of footsteps on the bedroom floor.
Finishing the page, he sets his book
on the arm of the living room chair
and rises as she enters the room.

His arms and his heart open wide.
She allows him to envelop her as
he strokes the small of her back.
Their bodies remember each other
like a favorite meal after a long fast.

Breast Cancer Poem

It's not like removing a bullet in the old west,
where the whiskey-soaked doc drops
the lead fragment—clank—into a silver tray
and says, "Got it. You're gonna make it,
young feller."

This seems more exorcism than extraction.
When it's over they wheel you through sliding
glass doors as somewhere a clock starts
counting back from five years.

We step into a future as fragile as new lake ice,
black water sleeps beneath us like a hungry
Grendel. We hold hands; take cautious steps,
listen through our feet for the crack or creak
that might tell us the moment he wakes,
ready to draw us under. But all is silent.

In time our stride smooths.
We no longer look down.
Our grip loosens; the grasp is lighter.
I notice how well our hands fit together,
no fumbling as with a stranger.

When we pause, my index finger traces
yours out to where its curved shore meets
the cool lake smoothness of your fingernail,
following it to the sharp edge, going over,
flowing under, until your finger closes
around mine, and we keep walking.

Lake Superior

So blue on this sun-drenched afternoon,
you'd swear the big lake has drained the
pigment from the sky, leaving
the old dome pale with envy.

Sleeping Alone

I'm teaching myself not to miss you
as I climb into bed each night.
I'm learning how to be alone
as I lean over to turn off the light.

Sleeping alone is an acquired taste,
I have the whole bed and plenty of space,
but I'd trade it all for the heat of your body,
I'd trade it all for the sound of your breath.

In Lieu of Flowers

Just yesterday
we welcomed his first-born son.
Just yesterday
we drank and danced at his wedding.
Just yesterday
he came to us fresh and new
through this same rich earth
that takes him back today.

I'm sorry.
I am not yet ready to say,
"Oh, he has gone on
to a better place."
The pain of his leaving is just too
fresh, too sharp, like the knife that
slides through flesh stopped
only by bone, leaving an ache
so deep it lodges in our very being.

I'm sorry.
I am too angry to accept
some master plan in which
the green is burned and
the brown left in the field.
Where all our graying wisdom
adds up to no reason
why it is our season to live
and his to die.

I'm sorry.
I do not know how those closest
to him will go on, but I know they will
for one thing is certain—

all of us must leave what we love
and what we love will someday
leave us.

John says Jesus himself cried at the
tomb of Lazarus.
Let us join our sorrow together
like the springs that weep from rocks
and hillsides to create a powerful stream
that carries his spirit. Let us celebrate
the gift he gave us
in his too-short presence here among us.

IV.

Small Regrets

My white feet glow
in the sun-filled water

as I dangle my legs
from the dock.

Tiny minnows, like small
regrets, nibble at my toes.

I move my feet and
the minnows scatter,

only to return just as
quickly. Tell me, what

is it that brings them
back again and again?

Fall Risk

I.
I find myself looking down. It seems my foot—
the left one—has acquired a mind of its own.
With concern in her voice, my niece says,
"Uncle, I think you're having a stroke."
"Nah," I reply. "I'll walk it off."

II.
By the time we reach the hospital my left arm
has joined the conspiracy. I'm pushed through
the ER in a wheelchair. It's packed
with hurting people. Bored people. Scared faces.
I feel guilty cutting ahead.

I'm parked in an ICU. Nurses and attendants
drift in and out monitoring vitals. I'm peppered
with questions like, do I have numbness or tingling?
They instruct me to close my eyes and raise
my arms. Then snap! The wheels on the gurney
unlock. It's off for an MRI.

III.
A neurologist enters the ICU carrying an enormous
piece of film and clips it into place on a viewing
screen. Pulling a pen from his lab coat pocket, he
points to a small white dot. "There it is," he says
matter of factly, "There's your stroke."

Fortunately, the brain operates like an efficient
highway department. It has already begun to build
a detour around this tiny white obstacle that has
blocked blood flow within my brain. Already my

arm and I are once again on speaking terms.
Nonetheless, the verdict is overnight observation.

IV.
Lying on my back, winding through hallways, it
occurs to me that hospitals are missing an opportunity
by leaving ceiling panels utterly blank. Here we are,
captive patients, positioned to take in whatever a
hospital may wish to share. Weighty messages:
"Care that Never Quits." "Keeping You Moving
For Life." And singular messages: "Don't
forget your flu shot!" "Do you have a completed
healthcare directive?" So many possibilities.

V.
We make a 90-degree turn and pass through a doorway.
The gurney stops. The wheels lock. We have arrived at
my room. The nurse asks, "How's your leg?"
"Feels fine," I reply. In hindsight, I realize my assessment
was somewhat misleading...at least incomplete.
I wasn't actually feeling much of anything.

With the attendant's help, I easily shift my hips
to a sitting position. And then, with one small step,
I drop into a crumpled heap on the floor. Lifting me
from under each arm, the nurse and the attendant
hoist me up and guide me onto the bed. When the
nurse returns a short time later, she clips a yellow
plastic band onto my wrist. It reads: *Fall Risk*.
The immediate implication: no solo bathroom trips.

VI.
It's been nearly a decade since my stroke.
Out of the hospital in just three days
with near full use of my leg.

The yellow bracelet? It's a reminder
I keep in the upper right drawer of my desk.

Being a fall risk is not limited
to the physical realm.
Most of us have tripped-up or stumbled
in a relationship or life planning, parenting
or decision-making, or in a myriad of life's dimensions.

It may mean we overlooked a blind spot,
overestimated or underestimated our competence.
The result? We're in a crumpled heap on the floor.
Having something nearby to remind us—
occasionally trying it on for size—can be helpful indeed.

Sailing Alone *

In calm water, under a clear sky, he
unexpectedly fell from their boat.
She extended her body, unfurling the tightly
curled ropes that held their memory
even as they entered the water.
But still, he slipped beneath its surface,
sliding between green panes of light
with a terrible sureness.

The patch of water now only mirrors the sky.
As she draws in the wet lines, droplets trail
from her arms and fall into the belly of the boat.
In the night, insistent waves lap against
the wood hull, sounding like a heartbeat,
sometimes a distant call.

Off the bow, the backs of dolphins crease
the water like molten silver.
Someone told her, it will get easier with time,
but she is not sure that easier is what she desires.
She has come to know where the sun sets and rises.
That is enough for now.

* Lisa. As this poem suggests, I have
huge respect for your mother. I, too,
lost my spouse. It's an experience
unlike any other.
I lost my wife after a long bout w/ cancer.
Your family lost your dad so un-
expectedly. That's a whole other challenge!
Lisa, I hope the three of you will
always be there for one another.
— Bill

Indra's Net

Dreams drift down and settle like dew
on your rumpled comforter decorated
in blue ponies trailing long, wavy manes.
A pulsing chorus of snowy crickets rides in
bareback on breezes of fresh-cut grass as your
blond lashes flutter like small night moths.

I have spent so long thinking like an island,
moaning a single note, pushing away from
being held. Your presence has lowered my
hands and opened my heart to all that
connects each of us.

Like the intricate net of the Hindu god, Indra,
ruler of the heavens, it stretches infinitely
in all directions. Threads cross threads and
at every juncture—a jewel, each of our lives
reflected in all others.

Life in Present Tense

I am a prisoner of the present tense.

I travel this Latin country crossing
       rickety language bridges,
having left behind my limited worldly cache
       of past, past perfect, future,
and yes, future perfect tenses.

I exercise my constricted vocabulary,
       forcing it through a slender straw of time.
There is no yesterday as I describe my
       adventures in the marketplace.
There is no tomorrow as I plan my
       trip to the volcano.

I can only hope my Latino host thinks me to be
       some *Estados Unidos Bodhisattva*—
a man who has abandoned the trivialities of this
       temporal existence for life in an eternal now,
not just one more ignorant gringo.

Rock Chant

Dance on the rock.
Stay on fingers and toes,
body out from the wall.
Scuttle like a spider
from crack to crack.

Dance on the rock.
Believe in your partner.
You're safe.
You entrusted your life,
don't take it back.

Dance on the rock.
Listen to her through
your fingers,
she's telling you
where to touch.

Dance on the rock.
Taste your fear,
then let it flow out
with your breath,
and give it to the sky.

Night Birds

Night birds have retired.
Small bones collect
under the owl tree as
we wait for dawn.

I have sacrificed
the important parts
without a struggle and
for so little in return.

If only I had known
who I really was
before I became
who I am today.

Enlightenment

The cat chases a tinfoil ball across the slick tile floor,
scrambling between table legs and careening
broadside into a half-opened door.

Me? With the help of a therapist,
I chase the jagged words
of my long-deceased father
into the darkening woods of my childhood,
stumbling over gnarled roots
and bashing my head again and again
on the jagged bark of his disapproval.

Tell me,
which of us is the more enlightened creature?

Second Half

I used to schedule breakfast meetings,
sometimes three or four each week.
After all, I'm at my best first thing
in the morning, and getting together
seemed like a productive thing to do.

I seldom schedule breakfast meetings
anymore. If someone asks to meet,
I usually decline. After all, I'm at my best
first thing in the morning, and being alone
seems like a more productive thing to do.

Crows Over Disneyland

No white gloves,
no Mickey Mouse hats.
No pixie dust,
no Siamese cats.
Just oil-black feathers
fingering the air,
getting closer and closer,
close as you dare,
'til you feel the boredom
beneath the tight smiles,
then just flying away
and gliding for miles.

River Town Dawn

Fog curls from the peaks of shingled roofs
as droplets fall from eaves.
The golden dogwood bows deeply
under the weight of last night's rain,
touching its tips to the grass.
White catalpa blossoms, trumpet-shaped
with scalloped edges, mat the damp street
like discarded corsages.

The river town air drapes the face of morning
like a saturated cloth.
Nearby, a rooftop crow barks to rouse the sun
as a bearded man near the river sheds his cocoon
of tired blankets.
He will spend the day drying everything he owns.

Rain

The rain stopped hours ago
but orphaned drops
find their way leaf to leaf.

Man Overboard

How lost do you need to be
before you can be found?

No one heard him hit the water.
No one saw the confusion and
despair in his eyes as the distance
between him and the ship stretched
until it finally snapped, creating
two separate worlds.

At first a flash of fear and then
a calm he'd never felt.
So, do you yell for help,
or decide, this is what you've
been waiting for your entire life?

About the Author

Bill McCarthy spent the early years of his career as an award-winning film and video writer/producer, followed by 20+ years as a coach to senior leaders and their teams in Europe and the Americas. All the while, he wrote essays and poetry.

In 2006, Trilobite Press of Denton, Texas published his first chapbook, Past Sins. The chapbook became the 30th in the University of North Texas' annual series, *Contemporary Poets Reading*. A more recent poem, "Breast Cancer Poem #2," was published by *Main Channel Voices* and nominated for a Pushcart Prize. The poem also became part of the anthology, *Cancer Poetry Project*, which Midwest Book Awards named "Best Poetry Book of the Year."

As board chair of ArtReach St. Croix, a Minnesota non-profit arts organization, McCarthy was instrumental in broadening ArtReach's focus to increasingly include the written and spoken word. He also launched, *Take Me to the River*, an initiative that expanded the celebration of the arts along 52 miles on either side of the St. Croix River.

Bill McCarthy lives in St. Paul, Minnesota with his wife, Danette, and their herding dog, Kip.

CPSIA information can be obtained
at www.ICGtesting.com
Printed in the USA
LVHW080040251022
731286LV00004BA/14